W9-DFF-106

Where Is Stonehenge?

by True Kelley

illustrated by John Hinderliter

Grosset & Dunlap
An Imprint of Penguin Random House

For Jada Lindblom and Willy Graves—TK

For Meadow—mysteries are everywhere—JH

GROSSET & DUNLAP
Penguin Young Readers Group
An Imprint of Penguin Random House LLC

If you purchased this book without a cover, you should be aware that this book is stolen property. It was reported as "unsold and destroyed" to the publisher, and neither the author nor the publisher has received any payment for this "stripped book."

Penguin supports copyright. Copyright fuels creativity, encourages diverse voices, promotes free speech, and creates a vibrant culture. Thank you for buying an authorized edition of this book and for complying with copyright laws by not reproducing, scanning, or distributing any part of it in any form without permission. You are supporting writers and allowing Penguin to continue to publish books for every reader.

The publisher does not have any control over and does not assume any responsibility for author or third-party websites or their content.

Text copyright © 2016 by True Kelley. Illustrations copyright © 2016 by Penguin Random House LLC. All rights reserved. Published by Grosset & Dunlap, an imprint of Penguin Random House LLC, 345 Hudson Street, New York, New York 10014. Who HQ™ and all related logos are trademarks owned by Penguin Random House LLC. GROSSET & DUNLAP is a trademark of Penguin Random House LLC. Printed in the USA.

Library of Congress Cataloging-in-Publication Data is available.

ISBN 9780448486932 (paperback)   10 9 8 7 6 5 4 3 2 1
ISBN 9780399542404 (library binding)   10 9 8 7 6 5 4 3 2 1

Contents

Where Is Stonehenge?

In the 1830s, a group of four friends climbed out of a horse-drawn carriage. The ladies and gentlemen had come up with an interesting idea for the weekend. But now they were stiff and tired from traveling all day from London. Tourists often came to Salisbury to see the cathedral. It had the tallest spire in the country. But this group had planned a different adventure.

After resting overnight in town, they crowded into a small carriage and were driven across the countryside. They closed the blinds on the carriage windows so they couldn't see out. Why?

At the end of their journey, they would reach a very special place. They wanted it to be a total surprise. So, in a giddy mood, they traveled on in darkness. It was bumpy, and the carriage seemed to be going very fast. Finally, the driver pulled the horses to a stop and told the passengers to open the blinds.

Everyone gasped at what they saw! The carriage was parked among giant stones standing in a circle. Some stones had fallen on the ground and were broken. But the stones still standing were taller than three men . . . What was this strange and amazing place called?

Stonehenge!

Some of the standing stones had other huge stones across the top of them. They looked like giant door frames. It was hard to imagine how people could have built such a thing thousands of years ago. Many people thought it had to be made by giants or by magic.

The tourists stood awestruck in the middle of the circle. They had seen paintings of this place and read poetry about it. Being there in person was very different. Even in a group of friends, there was a feeling of loneliness. There was not a tree in sight. The almost-flat land seemed to go on forever. The circle of stones appeared to jut out from the emptiness around them.

The wind blew cold, and gray clouds raced across the sky. Even with the wind, it was very quiet. Quiet and mysterious.

People have wondered about Stonehenge for more than a thousand years. How old is it? Where did the stones come from? Who built it and why? And *how*?

Unlike the Great Pyramids of Egypt, which are almost as old, there is no ancient written record of Stonehenge. But like the Great Pyramids, we know Stonehenge must have been important to ancient people because it took such great effort to build.

Now, with modern technology, archaeologists have learned almost as much in the last fifteen years as they knew for centuries before. (Archaeologists study objects from the past to find out about the people of long ago.) But many mysteries still remain. Those mysteries make Stonehenge one of the most fascinating places in the world.

CHAPTER 1
Circles of Stones

In the south of England, about ninety miles west of London, sits the Salisbury Plain. It is a lonely-looking area. There are few trees. Not much grows except grass. Few creatures live there except sheep. Yet the Salisbury Plain is famous. Well over a million people travel there every year. They come from all over the world to visit one of the great monuments of the ancient world—the stone circle called Stonehenge.

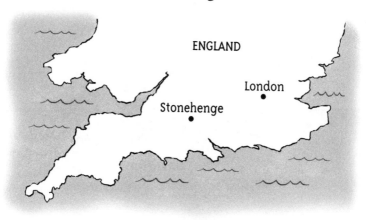

Stonehenge sits at the top of a slight slope. Because the Salisbury Plain is so bare, Stonehenge can be seen from miles away. Lichen-covered stones seven feet wide and fourteen feet tall form a huge circle about one hundred feet across. That's as wide as two basketball courts. The stones are a hard brown sandstone called sarsen. The sarsen stones were carved so that they are narrower at the top. This makes them look even taller than they really are. The stones are buried at different

sarsen stone

depths so that the tops are level with each other. Seventeen of these stones still stand. Many others have fallen and lie about on the ground.

Connecting some of the standing sarsen stones are ten-foot-long stone beams. They are called lintel stones because they are like the lintel, or crosspiece, of a door frame. At one time, lintel stones linked all the standing stones in the one-hundred-foot-wide circle.

sarsen stones
with lintel

Henges

The word *henge* is a very old word that means ditch, and there is, indeed, a ditch all around Stonehenge. There are several ancient henges to be found in Britain, but Stonehenge is the most famous.

Avebury henge

The circle of sarsen stones is what visitors first see. Inside that circle is another circle of stones. They are half as tall and turn bluish when wet, so they are called bluestones. There are only six now, although once there may have been as many as sixty bluestones. The bluestones were put up after the sarsens.

Within the bluestones, nearer the center of the monument, three enormous trilithons (TRY-lith-ons) stand with part of a fourth. Trilithons are sets of three stones, two upright with a stone across them. There used to be a fifth trilithon, but it has disappeared. Another mystery!

The largest is called the Great Trilithon. Only one of its standing stones is still upright. The trilithons form a horseshoe forty-five feet across. Inside the horseshoe are the remains of another horseshoe of six-foot-high bluestones.

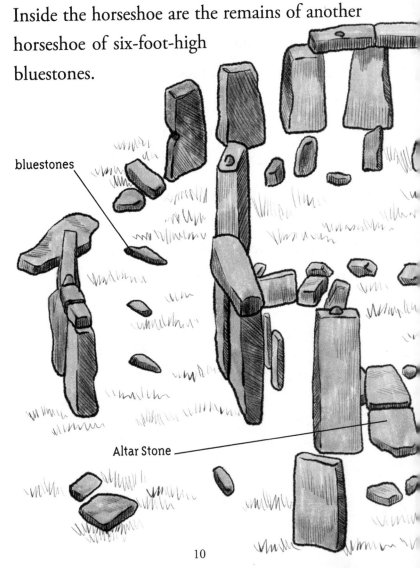

bluestones

Altar Stone

And finally, in the very center, is a sixteen-foot-long slab of gray-green sandstone. It lies flat and broken in two pieces. At one time archaeologists thought it was used as an altar in ceremonies. So it is called the Altar Stone. But like so much about Stonehenge, that is not at all certain. More likely, it was a standing stone that simply fell over.

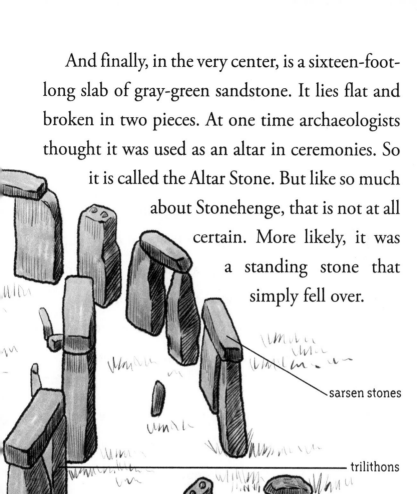

sarsen stones

trilithons

Ka-Boom!

In January 1797, a sudden thaw melted the frozen ground. A farmer was plowing a half mile from Stonehenge when he heard a huge thump. One of the giant trilithons had fallen! It turned out it had been set in the ground only about three feet deep, with over twenty-one feet above. With so little of the stone underground and with the ground freezing and thawing for so many years, it's amazing it stood for so long.

In December 1900, a storm blew down one of the sarsen stones. Its lintel was thrown eighty feet and broke in half. Then, in 1963, another sarsen stone fell without warning.

All of these stones have been put back up over the years, but there are still many that have been left where they fell.

Around the stones is a ditch and bank with a thirty-five-foot-wide entrance, which is called the Causeway. Near it lies the Slaughter Stone.

This giant slab of bumpy rock got its name because it is stained red. People thought that the color came from the blood of animals or people sacrificed during ancient ceremonies. But now we know that the rock has iron in it. That's what makes it red.

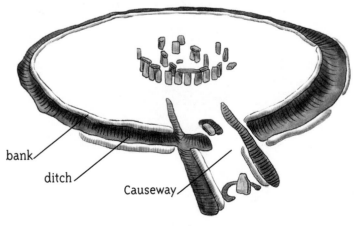

bank

ditch

Causeway

The Causeway leads to what remains of a wide two-mile-long dirt road. It is called the Avenue, and it curves down to the River Avon. Long, long ago, many travelers reached the stone circles from the river. As they turned the corner of the Avenue there would suddenly have been an awesome view of the giant stones.

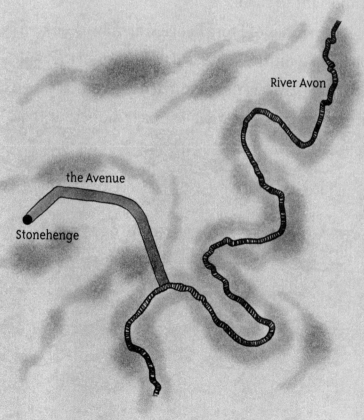

River Avon

the Avenue

Stonehenge

One important sarsen stone stands outside the stone circle in the middle of the Avenue. It's called the Heel Stone. On the longest day of the year, around June 21, the sun rises right over this sixteen-foot-high stone. The people of ancient times put it there on purpose. Marking and celebrating the longest day had to be very important to them.

The stones of Stonehenge still draw thousands of people on the longest day of summer. People are still in awe as they approach the stones. It's an amazing sight, but there is much more to it than meets the eye.

CHAPTER 2
Who Built Stonehenge?

Today we know that Stonehenge was built thousands of years ago. We also know it took a very long time to build. Many, many generations of people worked on it.

In 1966, archaeologists studied the area where a visitors' parking lot was going to be built.

They found several large post holes. The holes may have held posts from a house that was built as long ago as 8000 BC! The house was probably a single room with a roof of thatched straw. The land would have been covered with forests. Remains of pottery, bone, and flint have been found nearby. This proves that people were living near Stonehenge thousands of years before the monument was built.

Before 3000 BC, tribes of Stone Age farmers began clearing the forest. They lived in very basic wooden houses with white chalk walls, thatched roofs, and clay floors. Their clothes were made of animal skins, flax, and wool. They used stone tools and grew crops of grains and vegetables. The farmers kept animals like dogs, pigs, cows, sheep, and goats. They didn't have horses or any vehicles—like carts—with wheels. They had fires for warmth and for some light at night. They certainly didn't have electric lights ... They didn't even have candles!

Stone, Bronze, and Iron Ages

Prehistory means a period before there was any writing. This time period is divided into different "Ages" based on how people of the time made tools and weapons.

The Stone Age is sometimes called the Neolithic Period. It ended between 6000 and 2000 BC. Stone tools were used and also some copper tools. Bone and wooden tools were also used. Construction of Stonehenge began during this time.

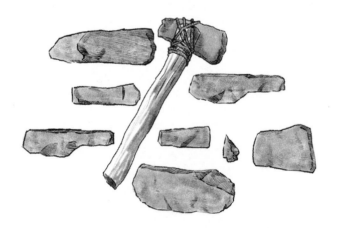

The Bronze Age followed, from about 2000 to 800 BC. During this period, people learned to make a stronger metal, bronze, by combining copper and tin.

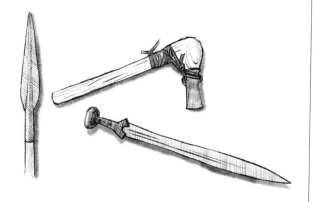

The Iron Age came after that. Iron is a hard silvery-gray metal. Iron tools and weapons could be sharpened, unlike bronze, which had to be melted and re-formed. The Iron Age in Britain ended around AD 40.

The building of Stonehenge began during the Stone Age. First, a circular ditch was dug. It had a six-foot-high bank. The Stone Age farmers had no metal tools. To dig the ditch, workers used deer antlers as picks and shoulder bones of cows as shovels.

Inside the bank was a circle of fifty-six holes, later named Aubrey Holes. (They are named after the archaeologist who found them in the 1600s.) They may have held wooden posts or bluestones as early as 3100 BC. Over time, early farmers added more wooden posts or stones. Perhaps it was for a wooden building with a fence. At any rate, this was the first version of Stonehenge. No one is sure exactly what it was for.

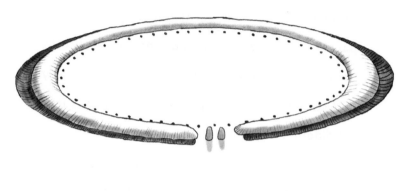

Then it seems that Stonehenge was deserted for hundreds of years—from 2900 to 2550 BC. After that, from 2550 until 2400 BC, people were using Stonehenge again. Archaeologists have found pottery, bone, tools, and cremated remains that date from this time. That's how they know Stonehenge was back in use.

Carbon-14 Dating

Carbon-14 dating was developed in 1947. It became one of the best ways to figure out the age of things that archaeologists find. Anything that is part of something alive, like bone or antlers, absorbs carbon. After death, the carbon decays in a slow way that can be measured. The less carbon that is left, the older the object.

The age of things can now be pinpointed to within 150 to 200 years. Objects can be dated up to 70,000 years ago!

After the early farmers, the next people who lived near Stonehenge, from around 2600 to 2000 BC, are known as the Beaker Folk. That's because of interesting beaker-shaped pots they used.

They also made weapons and tools out of copper and gold. As a community, they may have wanted to celebrate certain events together, like births and deaths. They may have wanted a place for celebrating the seasons or worshipping the sun.

We don't know what religion they followed, but they must have wanted a special place to hold important ceremonies. So they began to build the Stonehenge we know today.

First, before 2300 BC, the timber circle was replaced with eighty stones. Then, a circle of thirty sarsen stones and lintels was erected, and bluestones were put in place. An avenue was built to the River Avon, and the Heel Stone was placed.

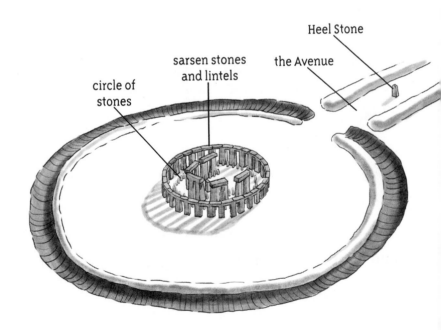

circle of stones

sarsen stones and lintels

the Avenue

Heel Stone

Between 2005 and 2007, archaeologists were digging near Stonehenge at the town of Durrington Walls. In a pasture, dodging cow pies and bulls, they made an amazing discovery. They found the clay floors of nine simple houses that had been there at the same time as Stonehenge, 4,500 years ago! There may have been a village with as many as a thousand houses! This must have been where the builders of Stonehenge lived.

Archaeologists found bones showing that the villagers had eaten a lot of meat and that feasts had been held. The bones also showed them that the people were well fed, because there was still some meat on them. A hungry person would have scraped the bones clean.

Studies of cows' teeth from the site showed that they came from many miles away. The cows must have been brought in just for the feasts. All this suggests that these occasions were

very important ones. Although people believe Stonehenge is most connected to the summer solstice, archaeologists have found evidence that it was also a place for celebrating in winter. They figured out that feasts were likely held midwinter, because they found teeth from nine-month-old pigs that were probably born in the spring.

Strontium

When people eat and drink, a mineral called strontium is absorbed in their bodies. Strontium can be measured in teeth and bones. Rocks and minerals in the ground have different mixtures of strontium. If the strontium in teeth matches that in the soil, it can show where a person or animal lived.

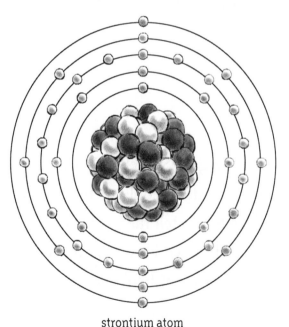

strontium atom

The building of Stonehenge was a huge job! The project needed people to figure out how to do it and leaders to tell the workers what to do. It took thousands of workers years and years of hard labor to complete. When one generation died, the next generation of laborers kept up the work.

The structure of Stonehenge did not stay the same. From 2300 to 1900 BC, the bluestones were rearranged many times. Stonehenge was rebuilt and redesigned and remodeled over several hundred years until 1600 BC. What we see today was made during this period.

After 1600 BC, people used Stonehenge less and less.

Around 1500 BC, life on the Salisbury Plain was changing. People were making better tools and weapons out of metal. They also were trading with people from other areas. Settlers from other places moved in, bringing new art, new ideas, and different languages. Perhaps these new people did

not care about Stonehenge as much. Or perhaps only a few important people in every generation had been allowed to use Stonehenge. In time, maybe there were fewer of these important people, and so Stonehenge was no longer used.

Another idea is that the climate got colder and wetter between 1400 BC and 700 BC. It could have become too hard to farm the land. So people may have moved away.

In 1159 BC, a volcano in Iceland erupted. Huge clouds of volcanic dust blocked the sun. It got cold. There would have been a shorter growing season. Also, it would have been harder to worship the sun if you couldn't even see it!

By the late Bronze Age, 1000 BC, farmers were plowing over old burial sites—and very close to the stones of Stonehenge. Stonehenge was now just an old ruin . . . unimportant and forgotten.

CHAPTER 3
Wrong and Wrong Again!

The first known writing about Stonehenge, dated around AD 1130, tells the story of a king who wanted to build a memorial to honor three hundred soldiers who were killed in a battle. He asked Merlin, the famous magician, to help. It was said that Merlin brought the stones from Ireland around the fifth century. Merlin then made himself twenty feet tall and lifted the cross-stones into place. Nothing to it!

Even if Merlin had real magic powers, he could not have built Stonehenge. According to legend, he lived thousands of years after Stonehenge was completed.

There are lots of other stories about Stonehenge that were once held to be true and are just plain wrong!

For instance, people used to think that Stonehenge was built as a Roman temple. England was once part of the ancient Roman Empire.

The Romans worshipped many gods and built many temples for them. But the ancient Romans cannot take credit for Stonehenge. Through carbon dating, we now know Stonehenge was already a ruin for thousands of years before the Romans came to England around AD 40.

If you ask who built Stonehenge, many people will say the druids. The druids were mystics, poets, and priests, who lived in Britain during the Iron Age. They believed that nature was sacred or holy. To archaeologists of the late 1600s and early 1700s, the layout of Stonehenge suggested that it had been built by people who respected nature. The druids fit that description. So Stonehenge must have been built by them. Right?

Wrong again! There is no connection between the druids and the people who built Stonehenge. Although they probably used Stonehenge at some point, the original druids lived two thousand years after Stonehenge was built.

Druid Ceremonies at Stonehenge

The archaeologist William Stukeley wrote a book about the druids. He thought they had built Stonehenge. His book inspired a group in 1781. They called themselves the Ancient Order of the Druids. They visited Stonehenge for the first time in 1905. They held a ceremony to bring in new members. A crowd watched as almost a thousand blindfolded men were led into the center of Stonehenge by druids carrying poles and wearing white robes and fake beards. It sounds odd, but they were very serious and attracted a huge following.

Today groups of druids still return to Stonehenge every year. Some of them wear robes or masks. With drums and gongs and dancing, they celebrate nature and the return of the sun. Others sit quietly and meditate. In a way it's nice that Stonehenge is more than just a tourist attraction.

It took archaeologists many years to figure out who actually did build Stonehenge. It wasn't until the 1900s that the real age of Stonehenge was determined. Once that was discovered, many earlier ideas had to be abandoned. And finally, credit for the construction of Stonehenge was given to the Stone Age builders.

UFOs?

Thousands of UFO sightings have been reported at Stonehenge. Ufologists say aliens visit it more than any place on earth. In 1954, a beam of light appeared to rise from the center of Stonehenge. A report in 1968 described a strange object that shot straight up from a ring of fire among the stones. A 1977 video recorded lights in a line over Stonehenge. They hovered and changed direction suddenly. Many strange Stonehenge events continue to be recorded on people's cell phones.

What do you think?

CHAPTER 4
Special Stones

Nothing about Stonehenge is simple to figure out. For instance, all those giant stones. Where did they come from? At one point, there may have been over 160 of them. Were they just laying around nearby?

Most likely not. They probably came from far away. We think this because bluestone isn't often found on the chalky Salisbury Plains, and sarsen stone is very uncommon there.

So special stones were brought to Stonehenge.

Why would anyone bother to bring all these huge stones from far away? Especially since moving anything heavy was so difficult back then? Thousands of years ago, when Stonehenge was built, there were no machines or even metal tools.

People didn't have horses or oxen. It would have taken a lot of manpower to move giant stones.

Today, the most common belief is that the sarsen stones came from about twenty miles north of Stonehenge. The heaviest of these stones was thirty feet long and weighed forty-five tons! (That's as much as a humpback whale!) They were probably too heavy to be moved on log rollers. Possibly, they were dragged on heavy wooden sleds, perhaps on greased wooden rails. Some steep slopes were in the way. It must have taken a long time and a lot of strong men to get the stones up and down those hills.

Even more surprising is where the bluestones probably came from—the Preseli Mountains in Wales. That is about 140 miles away from Stonehenge! Bluestones had special meaning for the ancient people. They may have believed that the bluestones had healing powers. The first farmers on the Salisbury Plain may have come from Wales and known about the stones and their powers.

The Preseli Mountains in Wales

Early shepherds on the Salisbury Plain thought the stones were magic. They thought that by scraping the stones and then throwing water on the stone dust, sores and wounds would heal. Even today some people believe Stonehenge is a place of healing. Hopefully, they don't scrape off any more stone!

The bluestones from Wales would have been brought across the sea and down the River Avon and then dragged over land for miles. That's hard to believe! Also, it's unlikely that boats of the time could carry such heavy stones.

In 1999, some experts believed this whole long journey was impossible. A bluestone that wasn't from the monument did turn up near Stonehenge. So maybe the Stonehenge bluestones were only brought from a few miles away. And maybe there were no other stones of this kind nearby because they were all used at Stonehenge.

However, in 2011, geologists finally proved that the source of the bluestones was, indeed, Wales. This fact left everyone puzzling over how it was possible.

Sometimes answering one question leads to new, more complicated mysteries.

CHAPTER 5
Building the Circles

So the stones came from far away. That much seems true. Besides the question of how they were transported, there is another big question. How were the stones put in place without Merlin or giants? It is hard to believe ancient people could move the thirty-five-ton stones, stand them up, and then place huge nine-ton lintel stones on top of them.

Archaeologists have found stone chips and primitive stone tools at the site, so the stones must have been shaped right there. They found that holes for the stones were dug with a slant on one side. Perhaps wood rubbed with slippery animal fat was placed on the slant. The stone would be dragged to the hole and a log tower made to brace it. Long poles, counterweights, and plenty of strong men could slowly slide the stone down the greased ramp and into the hole. Then it could be pushed, pried, and pulled to the standing position.

The lintel stones across the top must have been even harder to put in place. Perhaps a lintel stone was placed next to two upright sarsens and then raised inch by inch with log levers, off the ground and onto a support of logs. The log support then had to be built higher and higher until the stone was level with the top of the sarsen stones. Then, in the most dangerous moment, the lintel stone would be shifted sideways and into place.

The lintel stones had two holes carved near each end. Two bumps in the standing stones fitted into these holes. That held the whole heavy lintel in place. In woodworking that's called a mortise and tenon joint. Stonehenge 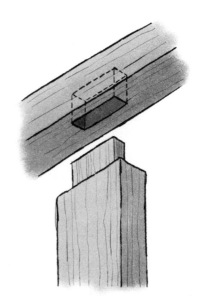 builders must have learned that method from building their wooden houses.

Really, these ideas of how Stonehenge could have been built are just theories. Guesses. New ideas keep popping up. One thing we know for sure: They did do it. So there must have been a very important reason to build Stonehenge—a monument that was in use for 1,500 years!

CHAPTER 6
So What Was It For?

Stonehenge probably was used in different ways at different times: for ceremonies of birth, life, and death; a place of healing; a feasting place; a graveyard; the center of sun or moon festivals; or as a calendar of the seasons. Perhaps it was built to bring together different people from all over England.

On June 21 every year, the sun rises over the Heel Stone in line with the center of Stonehenge. It shines through the double standing stones

inside, and light goes through the middle of the horseshoe of stones. Then the rays hit the Altar Stone at the center. This marks the summer solstice—that is what the longest day of the year is called.

The Avenue lines up directly with the mid-winter sunset. Stonehenge might measure moonrise, eclipses, or positions of the stars, too. Was Stonehenge a tool for astronomy, sun worship, or—more practically—used as a calendar?

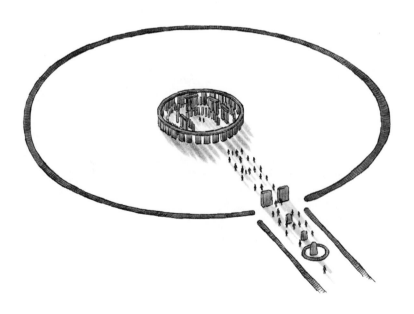

New clues about Stonehenge have been found in the countryside around it. Archaeologists are investigating the surrounding areas because too much has been dug away within the Stonehenge circle itself. There is a greater chance of finding important evidence outside the circle where there has been less digging.

Some pieces of the Stonehenge story have come from the air! There used to be a military airfield nearby. Photos taken from planes showed a pattern in the wheat fields below. That's how they discovered the long Avenue

from Stonehenge to the River Avon, one and a half miles away.

In 1925, a pilot saw white chalk marks in a plowed field two miles from Stonehenge at Durrington Walls. It looked like a wide circle—a lot like Stonehenge. He had discovered what came to be known as Woodhenge.

Woodhenge was built hundreds of years after Stonehenge. This circle had six rings of postholes inside a ditch. The holes held wooden posts that were perhaps twenty-five feet high.

Archaeologists wondered if the Avenue, Woodhenge, Durrington Walls, and Stonehenge were related to one another. They were all within a two-and-a-half-mile by two-mile area.

A group began to search for a connection in 2003. It was called the Stonehenge Riverside Project. It was Britain's biggest archaeological project ever. Hundreds of people were involved in it, including students and volunteers.

Archaeologist Mike Parker Pearson came up with some interesting ideas with the help of a friend from Madagascar named Ramilisonina. They think that Woodhenge and Durrington Walls were places for the living. Stonehenge, on the other hand, was a place for the dead.

Mike Parker Pearson and Ramilisonina

The project explored the Avenue from Stonehenge to the River Avon. They found it had been paved with flint . . . a very good road.

In 2005, they found a short avenue from Durrington Walls to the River Avon. This avenue lined up with the summer solstice sunset. A puzzle was starting to fall into place. Did this short avenue connect Durrington Walls to Stonehenge by way of the river? What did its link to the summer solstice mean?

In 2008, a new circle was found by the River Avon. It was eighty feet wide and may have held as many as twenty-five standing bluestones. It is called Bluestonehenge and is from around 2400 BC.

It seemed Durrington Walls was connected to Stonehenge by the River Avon. Perhaps people who lived at Durrington Walls brought their dead from Woodhenge, then along the river to Bluestonehenge; from there they'd go up the Avenue to Stonehenge. Since the Stonehenge Avenue lines up with the summer solstice sunrise and the Durrington Avenue lines up with the summer solstice sunset, the processions may have been linked to the seasons.

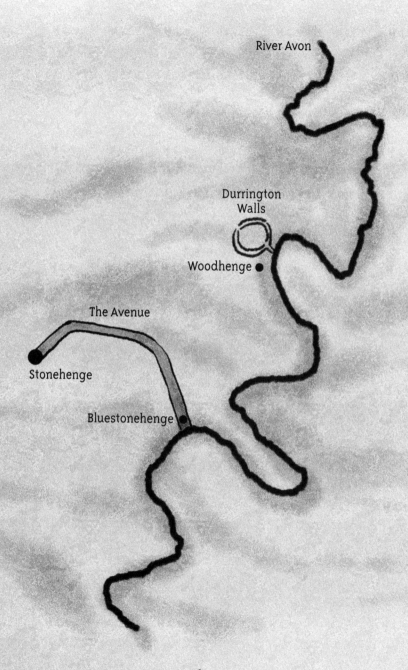

River Avon

Durrington
Walls

Woodhenge

The Avenue

Stonehenge

Bluestonehenge

Or Was It About the Moon?

A new idea is that maybe Stonehenge was meant to follow the moon, not the sun. The moon was important to ancient people since it was their main source of light at night. It was helpful to know when the moon would be brightest.

More discoveries are coming fast. But every discovery brings more questions. In 2010, another eighty-foot circle much like Stonehenge, with holes for wood or stone, was found. It's only about a half mile from Stonehenge. Over the centuries a lot was going on in this small area! Another recent theory is that Stonehenge was a cemetery. Human ashes were found in the 1930s in the ditch and the Aubrey Holes. More than sixty of these kinds of burials have been found around the edges of the stone circle and there are probably many more. Stonehenge may have been a burial ground in Britain for a thousand years. This fits in with Ramilisonina's and Mike Pearson's theories.

In 2014, there was a wild new idea. When a sarsen stone is hit, it rings like a bell, and the sound carries a long way. Could Stonehenge have been used to send messages or was it some sort of giant musical instrument?

With so many people trying to figure out the truth about Stonehenge, there are bound to be different ideas. Stonehenge keeps everyone guessing.

CHAPTER 7
The Early Diggers

Archaeologists, treasure hunters, and the curious have been digging at Stonehenge for centuries. And not only people. Rabbits, too! It's a problem for modern archaeologists, because so much of the site has been disturbed. Also, for a long time, good records were not kept of the things found.

In 1620, King James I visited Stonehenge with the Duke of Buckingham. The duke had his men dig a hole in the middle of the circle just to see what was there. They found horns, charcoal, bones, and even some rusted armor.

So the king asked the famous architect Inigo Jones to study Stonehenge. To Inigo Jones, it looked like a Roman temple, which we now know was a mistake. However, he did wonderful drawings of the site and published the first book about Stonehenge.

John Aubrey first saw Stonehenge in 1634 when he was eight years old. He never got over his excitement. He became an expert on ancient British sites. Aubrey was a careful observer and recorded what he saw. He put it all in a book. Aubrey is sometimes called England's first archaeologist. It was Aubrey who found the circle

John Aubrey

of what are known as the Aubrey Holes. And it was Aubrey who put forth the mistaken idea that druids built Stonehenge.

In the early 1700s, a local doctor, William Stukeley, loved Aubrey's druid idea. He got so carried away, he started dressing like an ancient druid and worshipping as he thought they had.

He may sound odd, but Stukeley made important discoveries. He was careful with measuring and recording his finds. It was Stukeley who came up with the idea that one of Stonehenge's entrances marked the sunrise.

In 1723, near Stonehenge, Stukeley discovered a pair of ditches two miles long, raised in the center. He called it the Cursus, a Latin word for race course. Stukeley imagined Roman chariots racing there. Of course, he was wrong about that. Still, we are not sure, almost three hundred years later, what it was for. A parade road? A playing field?

We know that it may have been built even before Stonehenge. In 2006, a pick made from an antler was found in one of the ditches. It was dated to 3500 BC, four hundred years before Stonehenge.

William Stukeley also dug in burial mounds nearby. Stukeley thought kings and their treasure might be buried under them. In the first mound he found a human skeleton. The next one had a javelin head, a red clay urn with burned bones, and ornaments and beads. Stukeley wanted to protect his finds . . . so he reburied them all! Later archaeologists found them again but could make little sense of them.

Burial mound

In the early 1800s, a wool merchant named William Cunnington dug at and around Stonehenge. With a crew, he discovered more than two hundred burial mounds near Stonehenge.

William Cunnington

They held bones, ashes, a bronze dagger point, a broken urn, and stone chips. Everywhere they dug, they left a metal token with the year and their initials, so that future diggers would know they had already been there.

A Gift

Cunnington left a bottle of port wine under the Slaughter Stone for future diggers. It was found a hundred years later in 1920. But the cork had rotted and the bottle was almost empty.

In one of the mounds Cunnington's team found gold! There was a skeleton and a gold decorated dagger, a gold belt hook, and two small diamond-shaped pieces of gold. This skeleton must have once been an important man.

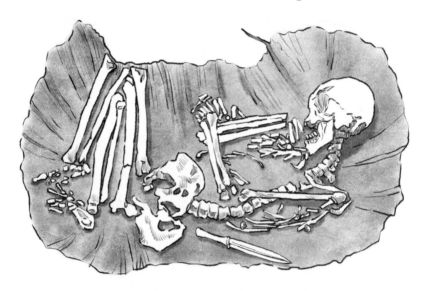

In 1802, Cunnington and his team dug up stag horns, burned wood, bones, and pottery right in front of the Altar Stone. A very odd assortment of other things turned up in the mounds: weapons, beads, buttons, a goose skeleton, and beaver teeth!

Cunnington didn't know what to do with all this stuff. He had shelves piled high in a house in his garden. There seemed to be no way to organize it all. It was hopelessly confusing!

All these early diggers felt the same way. Would anyone ever be able to make sense of this mysterious place?

CHAPTER 8
More Discoveries
and More Confusion

By 1901, some of the stones were leaning dangerously and had to be propped up with wood. One stone in particular looked like it was ready to fall. William Gowland was the archaeologist in charge of straightening that stone.

The stone was braced. Then a series of trenches was carefully dug under it in order to make a concrete base. A crowd gathered to watch the dig. They thought Gowland might find treasure.

William
Gowland

He didn't, but he made other interesting discoveries. The upper layer of dirt had stone chips, pieces of broken glass and pottery, clay pipe stems, pins, buttons, and some Roman coins . . . a layer of stuff left by tourists.

It got more exciting as he dug deeper. Gowland found the original holes for the stones and stone tools left by the builders of Stonehenge: hammers, mauls, shapers, and deer antlers. Deep down they found traces of bronze that dated the site from the beginning of the Bronze Age, about 1800 BC. For the first time it was possible to make a good guess about the age of Stonehenge. Also, now it was possible to figure out how the holes had been dug and how the rock was shaped.

Colonel William Hawley

Colonel William Hawley was Gowland's assistant. He took over the work from 1919 to 1926. He was the one who found an empty bottle of wine left by Cunnington under the Slaughter Stone. Hawley discovered some new post holes. But Hawley's work turned out to be a disaster. He kept poor records. He worked alone and was careless. He dug in the Aubrey Holes and at the base of each stone that needed to be straightened. Mostly he was finding chips and shards until he came upon a jumbled skeleton with no arms or legs and part of a padlock. Maybe it had been a prisoner, but why was it here?

Other Skeletons at Stonehenge

A skeleton of a man was found in 1923. He was about thirty years old and had been beheaded in medieval times. Could he have been a criminal?

In 1978, on the edge of a trench, scientists found the feet of a human skeleton from the Beaker period. It was the skeleton of a young man with tips of arrowheads still stuck in his ribs. It had been a violent death. He became known as the Stonehenge Archer because he wore an archer's wrist guard and arrowheads were buried with him.

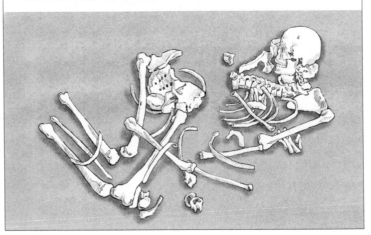

Hawley said, "The more we dig, the more the mystery appears to deepen."

He was getting tired of finding things. He didn't know what to do with all of it, so, just like Stukeley before him, he reburied a lot of it. By 1926, he had dug up half the site, and thankfully he stopped.

The history of archaeology at Stonehenge gets mixed reviews. Although many discoveries were made, many clues were destroyed before future scientists had a chance to study them.

CHAPTER 9
Tourists

The mystery around Stonehenge and the amazing sight of the ruins have attracted tourists for centuries.

In 1953, Professor R. J. C. Atkinson was photographing graffiti carved on the stones by visitors in the 1600s. He found something much more amazing. On the stone, he found very

weathered pictures of four axes and a short dagger. A couple of days later, the ten-year-old son of one of his helpers found more carvings. Fresh eyes could spot them now that they knew what to look for.

R. J. C. Atkinson

By the end of the summer they had found twelve carvings. In 2011, a laser scan found about 115 axe carvings and three or four daggers!

The axes pictured seemed to be prehistoric, from around 1600 BC to 1400 BC. But the carvings of the daggers looked like Greek daggers. Could someone from ancient Greece have come 1,500 miles to Britain and carved them? Could these carvings have been graffiti done by the first tourists to Stonehenge?

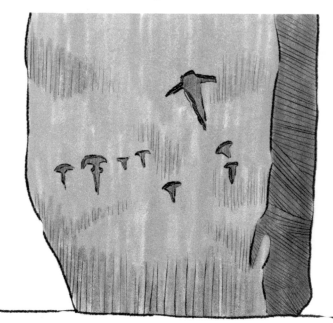

Graffiti at Stonehenge

When people visited Stonehenge, they sometimes wanted to leave their mark on the stones. Early graffiti found at Stonehenge was from the 1600s. The carving reads: "1oH:LVD:DEFERRE." A more recent deep carving says "H. Bridger 1866."

During the 1960s, people scrawled things like "Ban the Bomb" and "Free Wales" on the stones with spray paint. Now people are kept away from the stones to prevent more graffiti.

Even worse than carving graffiti was taking souvenirs. However, for hundreds of years, people hammered off pieces of stone. Usually, they took bluestone because it broke more easily. Huge chunks and even whole bluestones were carted away. What would people do with their stolen souvenirs? Some visitors believed bluestone could heal. Others thought you could throw a piece of Stonehenge stone in a well and get rid of snakes and toads!

Archaeologists were dismayed that people were stealing bits of Stonehenge right before their eyes. Not only that, treasure hunters were digging up the whole center of Stonehenge.

Of course, many people came just for fun. Stonehenge became a popular place for outings and picnics. People came by horse and carriage. Visitors spent the day reading poetry, drawing sketches, and playing music. Kids liked to climb and slide on the stones. Adults made a game of

tossing coins up onto the lintels for luck.

Another reason people came to Stonehenge in Victorian times was to count the stones. It was said that Satan made it impossible to count the stones and come up with the same number twice.

As tourists started showing up at Stonehenge, local people saw a chance to make money. Local shepherds offered tours and stories in exchange for tips.

Around 1740, the first drink stand was set up
to serve the tourists. An old carpenter built a hut
against one of the standing stones and dug out a
cellar under a fallen stone to keep the drinks cool.

In 1857, a new railroad made the trip from London much easier. Soon Stonehenge was used for concerts and cricket games.

By the 1870s, colorful modern druids had made the summer solstice at Stonehenge the big attraction. By 1900, things got crazy around the solstice. Two to three thousand people came. They were rowdy and in a party mood. They climbed all over the stones and broke bottles on them. As the sun rose, they sang "God Save the Queen" and gave three cheers.

In 1901, the owner of Stonehenge hired a guard to try to protect the stones. He built a fence and started charging admission. In that first summer, 3,770 visitors paid to get in.

Owners of Stonehenge

Stonehenge had many different owners. At one time, George Washington's great-great-grandfather and his family owned Stonehenge and used it as a dog kennel!

Around 1900, the owner wanted to sell it to the government. His price was too high, and people in England became worried. What if a rich American bought it and moved it to the United States? In fact, a rich American, John Jacob Astor, *did* try to buy it. He said he wanted to give Stonehenge to the British Museum. Even so, his offer was turned down.

So Stonehenge was auctioned off, and a local man, Cecil Chubb, bought it on a whim. He didn't know what to do with it, so in 1918, he gave Stonehenge to the nation. He was rewarded with a knighthood.

Great Britain built an airfield nearby and handed

over much of the land to private owners in 1926. The land became a pig farm. Then a cafe was built. There was talk about building tourist cabins. But in 1929, the land was sold to the National Trust, a conservation group. Today, the National Trust still owns and protects Stonehenge.

Cecil Chubb

By the 1930s, Stonehenge was overrun by as many as 1,500 visitors a month. So many people walked among the stones, the ground turned to mud. People climbed the fence and tried to knock down a lintel. It was becoming harder and harder to protect Stonehenge.

For one festival in 1951, about 124,000 people showed up. After that, barbed wire was strung around the monument to protect it. It looked like a prison. Even this didn't keep people out. In 1969, a mob of two thousand solstice celebrators surged over the fences.

By 1984, thousands of people were coming to Stonehenge and staying for days. They camped out in nearby fields. Since 1977, no one had been allowed to walk among the ruins except during the solstice. Unfortunately, visitors still were not always respectful. They even sprayed purple paint on the stones!

In 1985, on the night of the summer solstice, police tried to keep people away from the monument. It caused a riot that was called the Battle of the Beanfield. Hundreds of people were arrested. After that, there were no more solstice celebrations at Stonehenge for years.

Even so, a million people a year were visiting Stonehenge. For some reason Stonehenge attracts all kinds of tourists with all kinds of ideas: people who think it's a time machine or an energy source, snake worshippers, worshippers of ancient Egyptian gods, ufologists. Millions of footsteps on the ground and millions of hands touching the stones only caused more damage. How could this be stopped?

The latest answer is to bus tourists in from a new visitor center a mile and a half away. People then are only allowed on the path outside the monument. The experience of standing among the stones is lost. Stonehenge has to be protected, but are these the best solutions?

Fortunately, the crowds showing up for the summer solstice have grown smaller and more peaceful. In 2014, 36,000 people came. In 2015 the number was about 24,000. Still, on some days

there are as many as 50,000 visitors to Stonehenge.

The caretakers of Stonehenge want interested visitors to come. Yet they also need to keep the place safe from those same visitors. Can it be done?

CHAPTER 10
The Future

One thing that fascinates us about Stonehenge is that it is so much more permanent than we are. Stonehenge has lasted five thousand years. It could easily last another five thousand.

The National Trust is trying to make sure that happens. A highway that came too close to the Heel Stone and across the Avenue has been closed and grass planted over it. They are working on returning the land around Stonehenge to grassland as it once was. There will be more birds and butterflies.

The new visitor center displays five life-size models of Neolithic houses. Visitors can see how the builders of Stonehenge may have lived 4,500 years ago. Visitors will appreciate Stonehenge

even more. And if people value Stonehenge, they will help protect it.

The Riverside Project and other archaeologists do very little digging now. In 2010, the Stonehenge Hidden Landscape Projects began using new technology. Ground-penetrating radar can see what is underground without any digging at all.

And a lot has been found.
Hundreds of Neolithic henges, burial
mounds, ditches, and huge pits! It seems that
Stonehenge was only one of many similar
structures in the area.

In 2015, scientists made an incredible
discovery at Durrington Walls. Under about
three feet of dirt, they found the remains of thirty
huge standing stones. Archaeologists call the
new discoveries "Superhenge." The stones were

placed in a C-shape facing the River Avon. There were also pieces of sixty or more stones nearby. The site appears to have been a giant arena, built more than 4,500 years ago, around the same time as Stonehenge.

As more discoveries are made, we realize that Stonehenge was never a lonely monument in the middle of an empty plain. It was a part of something much bigger.

With more discoveries, we are also left with more questions. People still argue about the purpose of Stonehenge, who built it, where the stones came from, and how they were placed. Maybe you have theories of your own. With the mysteries of Stonehenge, it is good to keep an open mind and wait for the science to catch up . . . if it can.

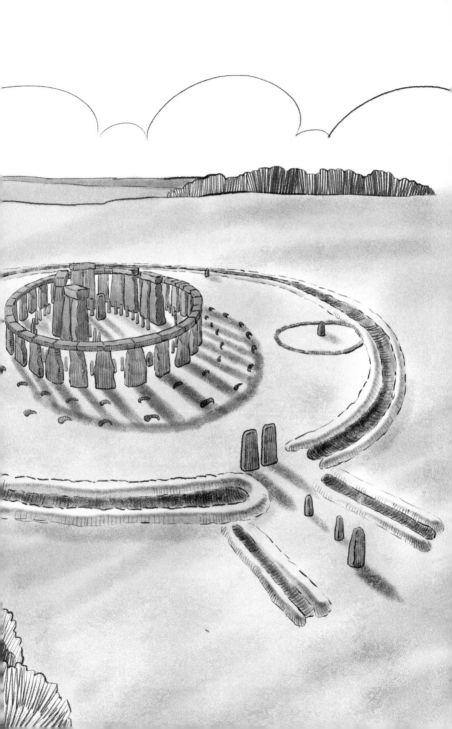

Stonehenge Copies

Copies of Stonehenge have been built all over the world, from garden ornaments to full-size replicas. One is in Maryhill, Washington, and is a memorial to soldiers who fought in World War I. One of the most famous Stonehenge copies is Carhenge in Alliance, Nebraska. It is called Carhenge because it is made

out of vintage American cars all painted gray. There have been playful copies of Stonehenge made out of cheese, refrigerators, french fries, carrots, candy corn, gingerbread, and snow. What do you have around that you could build a Stonehenge replica with? Maybe copies of this book?

Timeline of Stonehenge

c. 8000 BC	Post holes dug (under the modern parking lot)
3100 BC	Bank and ditch at Stonehenge; Aubrey Holes created
3000 BC	Timber structure built
2900–2600 BC	Stonehenge not in use
2600–2300 BC	Stones erected in line with solstice sunrise and sunset; Avenue built; timber circle built at Durrington Walls
2300–1900 BC	Bluestones rearranged repeatedly
1500 BC	Last known use of Stonehenge
AD 1130	First known writing about Stonehenge
1666	John Aubrey studies Stonehenge
1723	William Stukeley discovers the Cursus
Early 1800s	William Cunnington digs
1901	William Gowland restores monument and digs
1905	Modern druids hold mass initiation
1918	Cecil Chubb gives Stonehenge to Great Britain
1928	National Trust takes charge of site
1940s–50s	Richard Atkinson finds carvings on stones
1985	Battle of the Beanfield
2003	The Stonehenge Riverside Project begins
2010	Stonehenge Hidden Landscapes Projects begin
2013	New visitor center opens
2015	"Superhenge" discovered underneath Durrington Walls

Timeline of the World

c. 10,000 BC	Last Ice Age ends
2560–2540 BC	Khufu's Great Pyramid is built in Egypt
2000 BC	Bronze Age begins in Britain
c. 440 BC	The Parthenon is built in Greece
AD 43	The Roman conquest of Britain begins
1066	William the Conqueror wins the Battle of Hastings in England
1215	The British Magna Carta is signed
1588	Britain defeats the Spanish Armada
1648	The building of the Taj Mahal in India is finished
1776	Britain's American colonies declare their independence
1838	Queen Victoria is crowned
1885	The Home Insurance Building, the world's first skyscraper, is built in Chicago
1969	Astronaut Neil Armstrong walks on the moon
1994	The Channel Tunnel reconnects Britain to Europe
2015	Queen Elizabeth II becomes the longest reigning British monarch

Bibliography

*Books for young readers

Aronson, Marc, with Mike Parker Pearson. *If Stones Could Speak: Unlocking the Secrets of Stonehenge*. Washington, DC: National Geographic, 2010.

Ceserani, Gian Paolo. *Grand Constructions*. New York: Putnam, 1983.

Chippindale, Christopher. *Stonehenge Complete, 4th edition*. London: Thames and Hudson, 2012.

*Gray, Leon. *Solving the Mysteries of Stonehenge*. New York: Cavendish, 2009.

Malone, Caroline, and Nancy Stone Bernard. *Stonehenge*. New York: Oxford University Press, 2002.

Pitts, Mike. **"Henge Builders."** Archaeology Magazine Archive 61, no. 1 (2008). http://archive.archaeology.org/0801/etc/henge.html.

Price, T. Douglas. *Europe Before Rome: A Site-by-Site Tour of the Stone, Bronze, and Iron Ages*. New York: Oxford University Press, 2013.

Websites

clonehenge.com

www.english-heritage.org.uk

www.history.com/topics/british-history/stonehenge

www.archaeology.ws/stonehenge.html

www.bradshawfoundation.com/stonehenge/index.php